Don't Let the Peas Touch the Mash

and other poems

Elisabeth Sherriff

Copyright © 2023 Elisabeth Sherriff

All rights reserved.

ISBN: 9798379187828

To all the awesome, little people I have ever had the pleasure to meet.

CONTENTS

	Acknowledgements	i
1	Sometimes my Clothes Feel Itchy	1
2	It's Just What I Do	2
3	Don't Let the Peas Touch the Mash	4
4	Hugs	6
5	My Happy Place	8
6	I Don't Want to Go to School Today	10
7	What If...	12
8	I Love You, Little Cat	14
9	It's Too Loud	16
10	Friends	18
11	It Stinks!	20
12	Melancholy	22
13	Gravy Makes Me Wavy	24
14	Mastery	26
15	Superpowers	28
16	How Long Is It?	30
17	Art	32
18	Playtime	34
19	Relax!	36
20	Awesome Me!	38

A humongous thank you to my ever-patient husband, to my wonderfully supportive colleagues and to all the encouraging members of the Suffolk Writers Group.

No pets or cuddly toys were hurt during
the creation of this book.

SOMETIMES MY CLOTHES FEEL ITCHY

Sometimes my clothes feel itchy,

My tee-shirt is just too tight,

My shoes are just too ouchy,

And my PJs don't feel right.

Sometimes my clothes feel itchy,

My sleeves feel far too long,

My trousers pinch my bottom,

And my pants just feel all wrong.

It's Just What I Do

I get angry,

I get stressed.

I can't help it,

It's just what I do.

I worry,

I cry.

I can't help it,

It's just what I do.

I find it hard to make friends,

I find it hard to talk to you.

I can't help it,

It's just what I do.

I do things I don't understand,

I do things you don't understand.

I can't help it,

It's just what I do.

DON'T LET THE PEAS TOUCH THE MASH

"What's for dinner, Mum?" I asked.

"Sausages, mash and peas," said Mum.

"Can I have ketchup?" I asked.

"PLEASE!" reminded Mum.

"Please," I replied.

"OK, sweetheart," said Mum.

"Don't let the peas touch the mash!" I said.

Mum sighed.

"What's for dinner, Mum?" I asked.

"Fish fingers, mash and peas," said Mum.

"Can I have ketchup?" I asked.

"PLEASE!" reminded Mum.

"Please," I replied.

"OK, sweetheart," said Mum.

"Don't let the peas touch the mash!" I said.

Mum sighed.

You can substitute any food items to suit you. You might not like broccoli touching your mash or beans touching your chips.

HUGS

Mum touched me,

She straightened my collar.

I didn't like it,

I told her off.

Gramps touched me,

He tickled my foot.

I didn't like it,

I told him off.

Dad touched me,

He gave me a noogie.

I didn't like it,

I told him off.

Nan touched me,

She smoothed my hair.

I didn't like it,

I told her off.

I hurt my knee,

I didn't like it.

Mum gave me a hug,

I hugged her back.

MY HAPPY PLACE

This is my happy place,

You're not allowed in,

Not Mum, not Dad,

Not Nan, not Uncle Finn.

This is my happy place,

Where I feel really calm,

I know that right here,

I will come to no harm.

My happy place is my bedroom,
Curled up on my bed,
Where I read or I colour,
To soothe my worried head.

What is your happy place?
Is it indoors or out?
Is it playing with Lego?
Or sitting on the couch?

Wherever your happy place,
I hope it works for you,
Finding your happy place,
Is a great thing to do.

I DON'T WANT TO GO TO SCHOOL TODAY

I don't want to go to school today,

I want to stay in bed.

My teacher won't be in today,

We've a different one instead.

I don't want to go to school today,

I want to stay at home.

It's too noisy on the playground,

And I'm always on my own.

I don't want to go to school today,

I want to stay with Mum.

We have to do a test today,

That doesn't sound like fun.

I actually went to school today,

It really was OK.

The teacher was so kind to me,

I had an awesome day!

WHAT IF...

What if...

> *it's too salty or too sweet,*
>
> *Or it's too hot or too cold,*
>
> *Or it's just too different?*
>
> *Will your bottom fall off?*
>
> *Will your head explode?*

What if...

> *it's too early or too late,*
>
> *Or it's too dark or too bright,*
>
> *Or you just don't like it?*
>
> *Will your head fall off?*
>
> *Will your bottom explode?*

What if...

> *it's too shiny, too gooey, too hard, too peopley, too sticky, too stinky, too big, too small, too scary, too high, too noisy, too far, too rough, too late, too wobbly, too wide, too sloppy, too floppy, too hurty, too tricky, too much?*

What if you try to remember your last 'what if',

Did your head fall off?

Did your bottom explode?

No!

So, tell yourself this,

When you're faced with 'what if',

Your bottom won't fall off,

And your head won't explode!

I LOVE YOU, LITTLE CAT

I love you, little cat,

You are my best friend.

You never, ever judge me,

On you, I can depend.

When I am worried,

You help me to calm down.

You snuggle up beside me,

And I begin to lose my frown.

You never ever laugh at me,

Or tell me that I'm wrong.

You never ever put me down,

With you, I can be strong.

Thank you, little cat,

For being my best friend.

I will love you forever,

On me, you can depend.

Of course, you may not have a cat. If that is the case, you can change the wording for another type of pet. But I am not sure that you can snuggle up with a goldfish!

IT'S TOO LOUD!

I said,

Can you turn the telly down?

It's too loud.

I said,

Do you have to cut the grass?

It's too loud.

I said,

I don't like the bus,

It's too loud.

I said,

Do we have to go to Tescos?

It's too loud.

I said,

Can you hoover the other rooms?

It's too loud.

I said,

I can't go in the classroom.

It's too loud.

I played in the lounge.

Mum said,

Be quiet!

You're being too loud!

Friends

My teacher says,

Mia is my friend,

But she didn't play with me today.

My mum says,

Yusuf is my friend,

But he went to football without me today.

My dad says,

Evie is my friend,

But she sat with Olivia at lunchtime today.

My nan says,

Ruby is my friend,

But she went to Molly's house for tea today.

My granddad says,

George is my friend,

He shared his sweets with me today.

Sometimes, it is hard to understand what our friends do. They may do something that we don't like, or we don't understand. That doesn't mean they don't like you. It is good to use our words in these situations.

It stinks!

What's that smell?

It's cauliflower cheese,

It stinks!

It's your dinner.

What's that smell?

It's the washing on the rack,

It stinks!

It's your clothes.

What's that smell?

It's my new perfume,

It stinks!

Dad bought it for me.

What's that bad smell?

It's the dog,

It stinks!

She trumped!

MELANCHOLY

Do you know what melancholy means?

That's right!

It means sad.

You know, you can't be melancholy,

You are not a melon,

Neither are you a caulie, nor a collie.

So, you see,

You cannot be melancholy!

Have you heard about picky Lily,

Who picked a lily,

In Piccadilly,

Whilst eating piccalilli?

Did you see the bare bear,

Fixing the leek in the bathroom?

I think he went bananas,

Maybe he lost his marbles!

Something smells a bit fishy around here,

I think they're getting up to monkey business.

That cost an arm and a leg,

Fingers crossed it's a piece of cake!

Autistic people often take words and phrases literally. Some may have an advanced vocabulary and great grammar skills.

Gravy Makes Me Wavy

Sometimes, food isn't fun,

Because...

Pie makes me cry,

Yolk makes me choke,

Peas makes me wheeze,

Cheese makes me sneeze,

Curry makes me worry,

Mince makes me wince,

Peel makes me squeal,

Tea makes me wee,

Sauce makes me hoarse,

Mustard makes me flustered,

Liver makes me quiver,

Butter makes me splutter,

Pineapple makes me whine-apple,

Fruit makes me toot,

Gravy makes me wavy,

And baked beans... just... make... me... fart!

Sometimes, food isn't fun,

But there is nothing better,

Than a plateful of tasty nuggets,

And oodles and woodles of yummy noodles!

Mastery

Dina knows dozens of dinosaurs,

Flo is fluent at flags,

Aubrey is an authority on authors,

Stan is a fan of stamps,

Victor values volcanoes,

Iris is into Inuits,

Kris is crazy about creatures,

Meg is a master of mechanics.

And me?

I rock at rocks!

Autistic people are often very good at remembering lots of facts about certain topics.

Superpowers

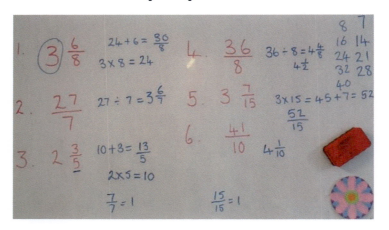

What are your superpowers?

I bet you have lots!

Are you **marvellous** at **maths**?

Are you **super** at **spelling**?

Are you **perfect** at **painting**?

Are you **great** at **grammar**?

Are you **fabulous** at **football**?

Are you **competent** at **computing**?

Are you **tremendous** at **tidying**?

Are you **remarkable** at **writing**?

Are you **natural** at **noticing**?

If there are some that I've missed,

Be sure to add them to the list.

HOW LONG IS IT?

What time is it?

About 9.

About 9? My clock says 9.03!

How long will dinner be?

About 20 minutes.

About 20 minutes? That was 23!

How long will you be at the shops?

About 2 hours.

About 2 hours? That was 3!

How long is that piece of string?

29.3 centimeters exactly!

Some autistic people like to be very accurate, particularly with numbers. Some autistic people are absolutely amazing at maths!

Art

Sometimes, I scribble,

Dark, hard lines on the paper,

It makes me feel better.

Sometimes, I take my time,

Soft, careful shapes on the page,

It makes me feel good.

My teacher says it's my gift,
I like that,
It makes me feel special.

My mum and dad say I'm an artist,
I like that too,
It makes me feel proud.

Playtime

On Monday,

Jack bumped into me.

I felt cross.

On Tuesday,

No one played with me.

I felt sad.

On Wednesday,

I stood with Mrs. Lacey,

I felt safe.

On Thursday,

I hid in the corner,

I felt lonely.

On Friday,

I played with Sam.

It was fun!

On Saturday,

I played with my brother.

It was crazy!

On Sunday,

I made a wish,

To play with Sam again.

Relax!

Lie on your bed,

Empty your mind.

Rest your head,

Relax your spine.

Heavy as bricks,

Relax your bum.

Heavy as trees,

Relax your tum.

Breathe in deeply,
Close your eyes.
Breathe out slowly,
Relax your thighs.

Count to ten,
Relax your nose.
That's too silly,
Relax your toes.

Heavy as trucks,
Breathe in deeply.
Heavy as moons,
Hope you're sleepy.

An ABC of Me

Being autistic is only part of me,

There's one zillion times more than a whole ABC.

I'm...

Awesome

Brilliant

Clever

Determined

Entertaining

Fun

Gorgeous

Humorous

Intelligent

Jestful

Knowledgeable

Lovely

Marvellous

Neat

Observant

Proud

Quirky

Remarkable

Skilled

Talented

Unique

Valued

Wonderful

Xcellent

Yummy

Zany

If I had to choose one word to best describe me,

That word is 'awesome',

That's plain to see!

Autistic people can be great at writing lists. Maybe, you could write your own list of words that best describe you.

Thanks for reading! If you have enjoyed this book, please consider leaving an honest review on Amazon.

Printed in Great Britain
by Amazon

22241536R00027